Knockout:

Knockout!

Rebecca Sjonger

James Lorimer & Company, Ltd., Publishers
Toronto

James Lorimer & Company Ltd. acknowledges the support of the Ontario Arts Council. We acknowledge the support of the Government of Canada through the Book Publishing Industry Development Program (BPIDP) for our publishing activities. We acknowledge the support of the Canada Council for the Arts for our publishing program. We acknowledge the assistance of the OMDC Book Fund, an initiative of Ontario Media Development Corporation.

Cover design: Meghan Collins

Library and Archives Canada Cataloguing in Publication

Sjonger, Rebecca
    Knockout! : how "Little Giant" Tommy Burns became the world heavyweight champion / Rebecca Sjonger.

(Recordbooks)
ISBN 978-1-55277-004-7 (bound).--ISBN 978-1-55277-003-0 (pbk.)

    1. Burns, Tommy, 1881-1955--Juvenile literature. 2. Boxers (Sports)--Canada--Biography--Juvenile literature. I. Title. II. Series.

GV1132.B87S56 2008   j796.83092   C2007-907517-7

James Lorimer & Company Ltd., Publishers
317 Adelaide Street West, Suite #1002
Toronto, ON
M5V 1P9
www.lorimer.ca

Distributed in the United States by:
Orca Book Publishers
P.O. Box 468
Custer, WA USA
98240-0468

Printed and bound in Canada

Contents

For Tim & Jane

1 Hard Knocks

It was a good thing that little Noah Brusso "would rather fight than eat," because he often went hungry. He was the twelfth of thirteen kids. There just wasn't enough food for all of them.

When Noah was born on June 17, 1881, the Brussos lived in a crowded log cabin near the sleepy town of Hanover in southern Ontario. The Brussos were so poor that Noah didn't even have a pair of shoes to wear to school. He had to sneak his church shoes out of the house or go barefoot.

Noah would have been in a lot of trouble if his dad had found out about the shoes. Like many parents at the time, Noah's dad ruled his kids with a whip. His mom once helped Noah prepare for a flogging in the woodshed by stuffing paper under his clothes.

Noah's school was no less violent than his home. About 75 kids in grades one to eight packed into the small stone building. It had just one room and one teacher. Kids who made trouble were sent into a dark closet or were punished with the strap. Even recess was rough. As an adult, Noah recalled "plenty of free-for-all fighting" at school. But he claimed that he "enjoyed boxing, more for self-defence than to hurt anyone."

Noah fought in his first boxing match when he was just ten years old. A

Noah's childhood school

tournament was held in a field behind the school. One of the youngest fighters, Noah won two bare-knuckle fights. That got him to the final match.

More than a hundred people turned up

to watch the final fight. Most of them bet on Sam Hill to win. Hill was bigger and heavier than the Brusso boy, whose nickname was "Lil Noah." But Noah moved fast to make up for his size. At first, he bounced around and dodged Hill's punches. When Hill finally hit him, Noah went down. But he pulled himself up and the boys went back at it.

Noah and Hill fought for over an hour. As they grew tired, Noah saw his chance. He punched Hill in the stomach and knocked him to the ground. Noah was declared the champion. It was his first step toward a boxing career, when he would call himself Tommy Burns and also be known as the "Little Giant of Hanover."

Noah did not have much time to enjoy his win. His parents were outraged when they heard that their son was boxing. Noah was not allowed to return to school. Instead, he began working in a factory. It was not what his parents had dreamed for him. His mom had hoped he would take up painting and become an artist. His dad wanted Noah to be a minister.

Noah's dad did not live to see any of his dreams for his son come true — he died in 1896. It was a huge blow to the Brussos. Noah's mom moved the family to Preston, Ontario. She found a job running a boarding house. Noah worked with blazing hot metal in a nearby factory. He

Dying Young

There were few ways for the poor to get help during the late 1800s. Death rates were very high. Without a proper diet, many people were weak or sick. Fast-spreading illnesses such as tuberculosis, a serious infection of the lungs, killed many people. Noah felt the effects of poverty firsthand. Five of his brothers and sisters died young.

Noah was 17 when he bought his first suit.

risked being badly burned, and he earned only 40 cents a day.

There still wasn't enough money for the family to live on. Noah's mom decided to remarry. It was the only way to be sure they would have a roof over their heads and food to eat. But her new husband, Hans Kuhlman, drank a lot and was violent. Plus he hated Noah — Kuhlman called his stepson "useless."

One morning, Noah was asleep in bed. He woke to the crack of a baseball bat hitting his skull, and a vicious beating from his stepfather. Kuhlman thought his stepson was sleeping in too late. Noah kept the beating a secret because he was so ashamed. He told friends that a dog attacked him to explain his bruises. But a scar on his face never let him forget what really happened.

Noah faced Kuhlman's drunken rage for the last time at the age of 17. Noah had just splurged on a new suit. When Kuhlman found out that his stepson had spent $40 on clothing, he roared, "Get out, and don't come back!" There was nothing that Noah's mom could do to help him. Noah was on his own.

2 Underdog Sports Star

Noah always had something to take his mind off things: sports. Noah was not only a great fighter — he was a talented all-round athlete.

When Noah was just 13 years old, he took third place at the Ontario skating championships. Cocky Lil Noah then challenged the world speed-skating champion to a race. Amazingly, the champ, J.R. McCullough, accepted the challenge. But he did not take Noah seriously. That changed when the race began and McCullough realized that Noah was a real threat to his title. The skaters passed the finish line within a second of each other. The champ barely beat the kid.

Noah's next rival was ready for him. Canada's speed-skating champ, Whit Hammond, challenged Noah to three races. The prize was a silver cup full of silver dollars. Noah agreed to the challenge.

A huge crowd watched the event. They bet on Noah, their hometown hero. Some people even tried to help his chances by toppling barrels into Hammond's lane. But Noah failed to win even one race.

The defeat did not slow down the budding athlete. Noah wanted respect — and he needed money. If he could get them through sports, he would do everything it took to succeed.

When Noah was forced to leave home,

he moved to Hespeler, Ontario. There, the 17-year-old found a job working in a mill. He also joined a local soccer team. He was great on the field, but he had a temper. When Noah knocked down an opponent during a soccer match, he was asked to join the town's boxing club.

Noah's boxing skills came in handy when he joined a lacrosse team in Galt, Ontario. Lacrosse was just as brutal as boxing. One of Noah's lacrosse coaches even used boxing gloves while training his players for the rough game. At first, Noah played goalie. This was meant to keep him out of harm's way, because he was so much smaller than most of the men on the field.

But Noah could take care of himself. The *London Free Press* claimed, "Brusso has never lost sight of the fact that hands were known long before lacrosse sticks." Noah became known for his punches as much as his plays.

Referees often threw him out of games for fighting. If Noah made it through a game with good conduct, he was paid an extra $50. Money always got his attention.

The team needed Noah's skill in the net. In his first season, one quarter of his games were shutouts, without a single goal from the other team. He rarely allowed more than two goals in any game. One team stopped playing midway through their match against Galt — they saw no point in staying on the field.

One of Galt's toughest games of the year was an exhibition game. It should have been fun, because the results would not matter at the end of the season. But Galt was up against a Native team called the Seneca Indians. At the time, most white athletes would not compete with athletes who were not white. Some of Noah's teammates refused to play. But Noah wanted to play the Senecas. He knew they were good. He told his teammates that playing them would help build up their own skills. They agreed to play.

The Senecas arrived with much larger sticks than the Galt team had. In protest, Noah's team left the field. But Noah did not leave his place in net. From the side of the field, Galt's team captain saw him there, ready to play. The captain decided to go back out, and the rest of the players followed him. The match was on. Both teams played a good, clean game. Galt won, 8 to 4.

Thanks to Noah's amazing saves, Galt became the Junior champs of Canada. They even crushed Senior teams. City newspapers noted Noah's skill as a lacrosse player. Hopes were high for his second season.

In 1899, Noah joined the Woodstock Beavers. His first game started out as a mess. Noah was pulled from the net after letting in two goals. The coach sent him out as a forward. When Noah scored, the coach decided to keep him on the field. Noah was ready — and so were his fists. He took on bigger players in match after match. He even knocked around referees.

Noah had some limits, though. He did not go after any player smaller than he was. During one match, Noah collided with a player from the other team. Noah jumped up, prepared to punch. Then he saw that his opponent was barely in his teens. Noah dropped his fists. He nodded and returned to the game.

In his third lacrosse season, Noah played for a team in Mount Forest, Ontario. He led them all the way to the Senior league finals. In the heat of a late-summer day, Mount Forest met Shelburne to decide who would take the title. The *Toronto Globe* described the game: "It was no namby-pamby ... contest, but a rapid, torrid struggle from start to finish." Noah's team lost the game by three goals.

But the Shelburne team was not done with Noah. After the match, a hulking player picked a fight with him. A Shelburne fan joined the brawl and cuffed Noah in the ear. Small and outnumbered, Noah took several hard blows. But it was nothing compared to the fights to come.

3 Into the Ring

In the autumn of 1900, Noah trekked to the border city of Sarnia, Ontario. The 19-year-old had a better chance of finding a good job there than he did in a small town. He soon got work that used his talents. Noah became a bouncer and broke up bar fights.

Noah was a better bouncer than he looked: he was just 170 cm (5 feet 7 inches) tall, and he weighed about 63 kg (140 pounds). One night, two men were drunk and looking for a fight. They attacked Noah, using pool cues as weapons. The news travelled fast when he knocked out both men.

Sarnia was just the first stop on a long trip that took Noah further from home. Soon he found work as a baggage handler on a ship. As usual, there were fights to be had. Noah did not get along with one of the ship's officers — no one seemed to. Like Noah's stepfather, the older man used his power to bully those around him. One day he gave Noah a nasty shove. Noah said, "Touch me again and you'll regret it."

The officer snapped a wet towel in Noah's face. "Put up your dukes, Brusso. I'm going to teach you some manners."

Noah reacted quickly. He punched the man in the face, knocking him to the deck. What came next was a one-sided battle. The officer got up and Noah knocked him down, again and again. Finally, the bully was out cold.

Noah lost his job because of the fight. They were docked in Detroit, Michigan, which became his new home. He quickly found a dockhand job. Within a month, he moved on to painting houses. It was not what his mom had in mind when she dreamed about him finding fame as a painter. But the money was good. Things were looking up for the young fighter.

He joined a local lacrosse team to keep active. He also began working out at the Detroit Athletic Club. As usual, Noah attracted attention. Sportswriter Joe Jackson suggested that Noah try boxing. "A fighter has to have the killer instinct and you've got it in spades," the reporter told Noah.

Joe set up a meeting for Noah with a fellow Canadian, Sam Biddle. Sam had once been a boxing champ, but his fighting days were long over. Now he owned a saloon and set up fights as a boxing promoter. Promoters paid all the costs of matches and then shared some of the profits with the boxers.

Sam agreed to help train Noah. They worked out in a rundown gym in the back of Sam's saloon. Day after day, Noah pummelled a punching bag with his bare knuckles. The goal was to perfect Noah's

The Colour Line

In the early 1900s, most white boxers did not cross the "colour line." They fought only white men. Title matches were off-limits for black boxers. In the rare bouts where white and black boxers did meet, the crowd often called out hateful insults, spat on, and hurled things at the black fighters.

punch and then unleash him on the boxing world.

In December 1900, Noah sat with friends in ringside seats, waiting for a match to begin. Jack "Tiger" Cowan, who was white, was about to fight Fred "Thunderbolt" Thornton, who was black. Thunderbolt had a great record. Tiger may have agreed to cross the colour line to improve his own standing.

Tiger approached the ring. He climbed through the ropes — and slipped. He sprained his ankle, and it looked as if the fight was a bust. The promoter, Mike Dolan, did not want to return the crowd's money. Six hundred boxing fans had paid to watch the match. So Dolan declared a challenge: "Tiger Cowan can't fight tonight. Is there anyone in the house man enough to fill in for him?"

Noah's friends thought he could take on Thunderbolt. But Noah was not so sure. He

Noah in boxing gear common in the early 1900s

was 12 cm (5 inches) shorter and weighed 13 kg (30 pounds) less than Thunderbolt.

Thunderbolt noticed the crowd around Noah trying to get him out of his seat. The thunderbolt-tattooed boxer goaded him. "Come ahead, boy. I won't hurt you — much."

Noah's pride drove him to action. "Fellah, do you want to fight me right now?" he hollered.

Dolan took Noah to the dressing room. The rookie suited up in borrowed shoes, trunks, and gloves. Boxers did not wear mouthguards at the time. Sometimes they tucked orange peels over their teeth, but Noah had no protection. Nervous energy raced through him. His first big fight was about to begin.

Boxers agreed on the number of rounds in a match before it started. Fights scheduled for 45 rounds were common. In 1893, a match went 110 rounds before it was called off by the referee! Thunderbolt and Tiger had settled on just six rounds. But no one expected the fight between the skilled boxer and the novice to last that long — not even Noah.

The gong sounded. Noah bobbed around in his oversized shoes. Tough and

Queensberry Boxing Rules

Noah and other prizefighters followed rules for boxing that were created in 1867 and backed by the Marquis of Queensberry. The 12 rules outlined the basics of the sport. For example, boxers were to wear new, well-fitted gloves. Footwear with springs was not allowed. Rounds were three minutes long. Between rounds there was one minute of rest. A boxer who was knocked down had ten seconds to get up. If he did, the round resumed. If he could not get up, the match went to the other boxer.

mean, Thunderbolt jabbed at Noah. A quick, sharp punch to the side of his head made Noah's ears ring. The blows kept on coming for two rounds. Then, in the third round, Noah caught a break. He landed an overhand right punch. Thunderbolt went down. By the time the referee had counted five seconds, Thunderbolt was back up and angry. But Noah was ready, moving fast and low.

The crowd was surprised that Noah made it to the fourth round. Even more surprising was that Noah knocked Thunderbolt down to the mat again. By the fifth round, the tide had turned against the black fighter. The fans wanted Noah to win. And he didn't let them down. Noah's upper body twisted and his right foot turned. His fist flew in a straight line to Thunderbolt's head. Noah's powerful right cross knocked Thunderbolt face-first to the ground.

Thunderbolt was down for the count. Noah had won his first real fight.

Just as ten-year-old Noah's victory over Sam Hill had turned sour, the thrill of this win was short-lived. Many people — even his trainer — were shocked that Noah would box with a black fighter. But Noah stood his ground and said, "I don't want to duck any man."

4 Nice Guys Finish First

Lil Noah was a prizefighter. As much as he loved boxing, he had no interest in being an amateur. Noah was in it for the money — and the respect. "I wanted to be more than just an average person. I wanted to be a somebody," he explained.

Noah was ready for a second match. On January 2, 1901, he would fight Billy "Battleship" Walsh. It would be tough: Battleship was half a head taller than Noah. And he fought dirty.

Half an hour before the match, a telegram arrived at Noah's dressing room. He read the message and began to weep. When Sam entered the dressing room, he found Noah in mourning. "It's my mother, she's dead," cried the boxer.

Sam knew that the telegram was a trick to upset Noah. "The Battleship sends that very same message to all his first-time opponents," he explained. Noah was so angry about the trick that he lashed out when he entered the ring. By the fourth round, Battleship was out cold.

Battleship stayed unconscious for at least half an hour. When he came to, he wondered aloud, "Did I lose?"

His trainer joked, "No, you won, but the ceiling fell on you once you got in the dressing room."

After knocking out Battleship, Noah thought that he might have a shot at taking the Michigan middleweight boxing title. But there was a glitch. The previous champ retired undefeated, and two fighters claimed the title.

Boxers were not ranked during Noah's career. There was no official body governing the sport of boxing — it wasn't even legal in many places. Champions were usually agreed upon by the fighters and the fans. Anyone could challenge a champion, who was the one who decided if he would fight. When undefeated champions retired, the title was up for grabs.

Most people thought that Ed Sholtreau was the true champ. Noah wanted to take him on. Sam Biddle advised against it, but Noah knew what he was doing. On January 4, 1901, Noah stepped into the ring to fight for the title. Noah showed off his punching power and knocked out Sholtreau just a minute and a half into the first round. Noah was on his way to being named champ.

Noah's next fight pitted him against Battleship Walsh for the second time. Noah held a grudge over the cruel trick that Battleship had tried to play on him. Anger fuelled Noah's blows. In the sixth round, he knocked out his foe again.

Just over a year had passed since Noah's first fight. Now Thunderbolt Thornton was complaining that Noah had just been lucky in his first big fight against him. Noah agreed to a rematch.

A lot had changed since their fight in 1900. Noah was no longer a nervous rookie called up from the seats. He turned down the $50 that the promoter offered him for the fight. Noah held out until his share was doubled. One hundred dollars was a lot of cash back then.

Tickets to the match sold out. Plenty of fans wanted to watch a white boxer cross the colour line. That night, a team of police officers stood around the ring.

Noah thought they were there to stop the fight. But the chief of police made a surprise announcement. The officers would not allow either boxer to be knocked out, to avoid serious injuries.

The first four rounds went by without the police having to get involved. Then, in the fifth round, Noah struck out with his right fist and followed with his left, knocking Thunderbolt to the ground. The referee began to count: one, two, three, four, five, six, seven, eight, nine … Thunderbolt got up just in time, ready to face Noah again. But the police enforced the new rule and called an end to the match. The referee declared Noah the winner.

Later that winter, Noah signed on to fight Harry Peppers, another black boxer. Sam worried that Noah was ruining his career by crossing the colour line again and again. Not only that, Peppers was downright dangerous. One of his punches had killed an opponent.

Again, law officials were nervous about the match. The white crowd would go wild if Noah lost. Lucky for the police, Peppers took a beating. He wanted out of the ring by the end of round two, and would not return to face Noah's blows.

Despite their uneven matchup, Noah knew that Peppers was a well-informed fighter. That night, Noah invited Peppers out to dinner to talk about boxing. However, the black boxer was not welcome at the restaurant where they tried to eat. Noah became so angry that the police had to be called. They forced the prizefighters out onto the street. Noah ended up taking Peppers home for dinner.

But Noah was not friendly with all his rivals. Like Thunderbolt Thornton, Ed Sholtreau put Noah's win down to luck. Noah wanted a chance to prove his skill.

In the spring of 1902, the champ agreed to fight Sholtreau again. Their rematch at the Detroit Athletic Club was scheduled for ten rounds.

Noah did well in the first few rounds. Then, in the fourth round, Sholtreau threw a punch that sent Noah to the mat. It was the first time he was knocked down in a prizefight. Noah was hurt, surprised, and scared. He struggled to fend off Sholtreau for the next six rounds. Noah just barely won the bout on points.

Noah headed to Lansing, Michigan, for his next fight. It was worth the trip: Noah added one more knockout to his record while he was there.

As Noah walked back to his hotel after the fight, he spotted flames blazing in the night sky. Fire was raging through a building. Noah saw a black woman and two young girls trapped on a smoky balcony two storeys up. He raced over to help them. The woman helped the girls one at a time over the edge of the balcony and Noah caught them. Then he ran into the burning building for the woman. Noah found her and brought her outdoors.

Win, Lose, or Draw

A boxer can win a match three ways. The match is won by knockout if the opponent is knocked down and does not get back up during the count of ten. If the opponent is not knocked out, but is too injured to go on, it is a technical knockout. If both boxers make it to the end of the match, the referee or judges keeping score decide on a winner based on performance. They may also declare a draw, or tie, between the boxers. Noah won 48 fights, had nine draws, and lost only five times during his career.

The family was safe, but they had nowhere to stay. Noah gave them his hotel room, and slept on a bench at the train station. It was a shocking thing for a white man to do at the time, but Noah knew how it felt not to have anywhere to turn for help.

5 The Undisputed Champion

At the end of 1902, Noah had one goal. He wanted to be the undisputed Michigan middleweight boxing champion. He had beaten Ed Sholtreau, but still had to take on Tom McCune, who also claimed the title. A fight was planned for December 26, Boxing Day. Noah and McCune met in the ring at the Light Guard Armory in Detroit.

Both men were wary during the first few rounds. Then the action heated up in rounds four and five. Noah knocked down McCune three times. McCune also knocked Noah down onto the mat. Neither boxer went down for the count, but they needed a rest by round six. They kept clinching — clutching each other to avoid being punched. Noah and McCune were so slow that the crowd turned on them. Jeering fans tossed trash into the ring.

Midway through the seventh round, a series of blows brought McCune down to the ground, but he rose before the referee counted to ten. Noah knocked McCune back down. With 20 seconds left on the clock, the referee declared that McCune could not continue. Noah was Michigan's middleweight champ. The 21-year-old appeared invincible.

Noah was the official state champ for just three weeks before he faced his first challenger. He agreed to fight boxer

Mike Schrek. Many people believed that Schrek would soon be the heavyweight world champ.

Noah prepared for the match with unusual workouts. He got bored doing the same routine again and again. A reporter revealed that Noah's workouts ranged "from tree-climbing to swimming in snow-fed rivers, and from sprinting up hills to horseback riding."

Weight Divisions

Boxers are grouped by their weight. There were eight weight divisions when Noah was a fighter: flyweight, bantamweight, featherweight, lightweight, welterweight, middleweight, light heavyweight, and heavyweight. The lightest boxers were flyweights. The rules and divisions changed often over the years. Today, there are 17 different weight classes!

But all his training did not help Noah with Schrek, who boxed left-handed. Noah had never boxed with a southpaw. No matter how he tried, he could not get to Schrek — even Noah's famous right-hand punch failed him. And Schrek had no trouble pummelling the smaller boxer. Noah toughed it out and lasted the whole ten rounds. But Schrek had scored the points for a win. It was Noah's first loss.

Joe Jackson wrote, "He was naturally nervous, in his first meeting with a man of reputation." Other sportswriters were not so kind. Even Noah knew that he had not fought as well as Schrek had. At least Noah did not lose his title. As a heavyweight, Schrek could not claim it. Only boxers from the same or lower weight classes could take titles from a champ.

Noah went back to Ontario and laid low after the defeat. He hit the ice and played some hockey. He also visited his mom. Worried for his safety, she begged him to stop boxing. But he wouldn't listen to her. After a few days, he returned to Detroit.

Noah and his trainer, Sam Biddle, knew there was work to be done. It took just one high-profile loss to ruin a boxer. Noah had to get back in the ring and win. But his next victory, over a light heavyweight, failed to impress people. So Noah made a stunning announcement. He would defend his title in two fights on the same night. It had never been done before.

Noah prepared to fight Dick "Bull" Smith and Jim "Reddy" Phillips. He had beaten both men before, but Bull and Reddy were tough. Whomever faced Noah in the second match had a very good chance of winning. Bull and Reddy flipped a coin to see who that would be. Reddy won the toss, so Bull was Noah's first challenger.

In round one, the boxers seemed evenly matched. But Noah had the upper hand by the second round, and it was all over in the third. Noah knocked down Bull twice in a row. A right-hand punch to the jaw took him down for good. The referee gave the match to Noah.

Noah was still the champ, but he had to beat Reddy. Noah had taken a hard blow during the first match. Reddy knew that he had the advantage, but he was not interested in a clean fight. At one point, he kicked Noah in the groin. The referee warned the challenger to follow the rules, but he wouldn't fight fair. The men boxed only two rounds before the match was called. The referee disqualified Reddy and handed Noah the win.

Noah's record was very good. Few boxers from the southern part of Michigan would step into the ring with him. So, he arranged a trip to northern towns in the state to meet new fighters. His first stop was Houghton, where Noah agreed to fight Jimmy "Bearcat" Duggan. Miners packed the town hall on the night of the bout. Bearcat was strong, but Noah had greater boxing skills. He pounded Bearcat's body. In the ninth round, Noah landed a knockout blow to his opponent's head.

Noah had defended his title away from his own turf. Now he was ready to relax with one of his favourite pastimes: poker. Noah spent the next two weeks playing cards. When he moved on to the next town, he was hundreds of dollars richer.

A skilled light heavyweight awaited the champ in Sault Ste. Marie, Michigan. Jack "Spider" Hammond's record of wins and knockouts rivalled Noah's. People expected a good matchup. And it was good — but short.

The *Sault Ste. Marie Evening News* reported that Noah "was in and out and around, ducking, dodging, and hitting with right and left so fast that it was impossible to follow the blows." He knocked out Spider with an uppercut in the third round. Noah had his coat on before the referee had even finished his count to ten.

Always the rebel, Noah fought two black boxers on his tour through the state. One of these matches ended in a draw — another new experience for Noah. But crossing the colour line was not his only defiant act in northern Michigan. Noah's girlfriend Irene joined him on the trip. Against her parents' wishes, they married on a whim while away from home.

Sam warned Noah that being with a woman would make him weak. The trainer wanted his fighter strong and mean. But Sam had no need to fear that a wife would distract Noah. The champ was back in action less than a week after he tied the knot. He added another knockout to his growing list of victories. By the end of 1903, Noah had won nine fights with only one loss and one draw.

The Canadian was generous with his prize money. Some of the cash was used to set up a boys' boxing club in a poor part of Detroit. Noah knew what life was like for the young men who joined. He wanted to help them.

The club did well until a black boy began boxing there. White parents were outraged. They would not allow their sons to go back to the club. But Noah would not kick out the black fighter, so the club shut down. It was one of the few battles that the fighter lost in Detroit.

6 Introducing Tommy Burns

On January 28, 1904, Noah almost killed a man.

That night he faced Ben "Gorilla" O'Grady. Gorilla was a brutal fighter who played mind games. When his opponent was in earshot, he would ask his assistants, "Shall I kill him? Which round shall I knock him out in?" As it turned out, Noah was the one to be feared. By the third round, the battle was fierce. Noah managed to sneak in a right cross. His fist hit Gorilla's jaw and knocked him unconscious.

Everyone waited for Gorilla to come around, but he didn't. His body was hauled to the corner of the ring. Smelling salts and cold water failed to revive him. Gorilla's team carried him to his dressing room. Soon after, they called out for a doctor, who had the fighter rushed to the hospital. Gorilla was in a coma.

The police charged Noah with assault. If Gorilla died, Noah would be charged with manslaughter. "If I've killed a man with these [hands] I'll never fight again, so help me God," he said while in prison. He was only 22 years old.

Noah was denied bail, as the police worried that he would flee to Canada if he was free. But they did allow Noah to leave jail to visit Gorilla in the hospital. After four days, Gorilla finally came to. But his injuries had left him brain-damaged.

Gorilla and his manager left the hospital without telling the police. A friend of Noah's from his lacrosse days helped sneak them out of the city. Without a victim, the police did not have anything on Noah, and dropped the charge. But Noah had to promise not to box in Michigan for a year.

The news of Noah's arrest made it all the way to Ontario. His mom was embarrassed and filled with fear. Once again, she pleaded with her son to stop boxing. If he did not kill someone, there was the chance that he may be killed himself. But Noah did not intend to go back to being a nobody. He made a plan. His mom would be watching for reports about Noah Brusso. What if he changed his name?

In Noah's day, many boxers used stage names. The boxer known as Tom McCune was actually Polish. If he could change his name and pretend to be Irish, so could

Noah. Noah chose the name Ed Burns, but it didn't feel quite right. After a few weeks, he decided to change Ed to Tommy. In the winter of 1904, prizefighter Tommy Burns was born.

Tommy had to leave Detroit. Chicago, Illinois, seemed like the perfect place for him to start again. The *Chicago Tribune* boasted that it was "one of the best, if not

We're all Irish!

Many great boxers were Irish, including world heavyweight champ Jim Jeffries. Fans came to expect fighters with Irish names to do well. Using an Irish name to conceal a boxer's nationality or a hard-to-pronounce last name was common. By 1916, there was a call to force boxers to use their real names. Promoter James Buckley complained, "Any man who [can't] get along with his own name [is] no good."

the best, fight towns in the country." There was also plenty of money to be made there. Chicago boxing fans were willing to pay for tickets that cost four times what they did for boxing matches in Detroit.

Chicago may have been new to Tommy, but there were some familiar faces there. At the end of February, Tommy met up with Mike Schrek again. Maybe Tommy's new name helped him, because his second bout with Schrek ended in a draw.

Tommy soon saw that Chicago was full of organized crime. The Italian mob, or Mafia, ruled the city. Even boxing was crooked. The Mafia bribed fighters to "throw" fights, or box to lose. The crooks then bet huge sums of money on the man they knew would win.

Before his fourth match as Tommy Burns, the young boxer was offered $1,000 to lose to Italian-American fighter Tony Caponi. Tommy had fought Caponi

Tommy was short, but he was also strong and tough.

before, and the bout had ended in a draw. Tommy wanted a chance to win the rematch. He turned down the money.

Someone was sent to convince Tommy to cooperate. He was told to fake being knocked out by Caponi, or his legs would be broken. Tommy bought a gun to protect himself and refused to throw the fight. In fact, he won the bout in six rounds.

Tommy realized that he had to flee or the Mafia would hurt or even kill him. He had no reason to stick around — he and Irene had divorced that spring. He decided to put several states between him and Chicago.

He escaped west to Salt Lake City, Utah. He set up a fight there with Joe "Kid" Wardinski, a heavyweight boxer. Kid was big, but Tommy still pulled off his fastest win of the year. In the very first round, he knocked out Kid with a left hook — a powerful sideways punch.

With time to kill after the match, Tommy settled into a poker game. Part of his winnings was the deed to an Alaskan gold mine. It was a time of gold rushes and dreams of getting rich quick. Tommy, as always, wanted wealth. And he wanted to put even more distance between himself and Chicago. With his new deed in hand, the gambling man decided to try his luck in Alaska.

7 Adventure in Alaska

Tommy was on a steamship that departed from Seattle, Washington, in the spring of 1904. He was on his way to Nome, Alaska, a busy mining town. Nome was no Chicago, but a surprising number of businesses lined the town's two streets. They charged a lot of money for their goods and services. Plenty of cash also changed hands in the saloons where gamblers spent their evenings.

On his first night in Nome, he went to

the Northern Saloon, looking for a drink and a card game. He had $500 to cover all his travelling expenses and mining supplies. With any luck, he would have even more by the end of the night. Tommy joined a game — and quickly learned that he was out of his league. Two girls sang and danced on the saloon's stage as he lost game after game.

Drunk and almost out of cash, Tommy turned his attention to the stage. He had always loved to sing, and had little to lose. Tommy hopped onto the stage and joined the duo of Lottie and Polly Oatley. The sisters took pity on Tommy and let him perform with them.

The next day, the sisters bought their penniless new friend lunch. When Tommy told them he was a prizefighter, Lottie and Polly knew how he could make some money. They thought a local boxer called "Klondike Mike" Mahoney would agree to a match, and it turned out they were right.

Klondike Mike had been a lumberjack before coming to Alaska. He was famed for his strength. Still, Tommy entered the ring expecting an easy fight. But Klondike Mike fought as if he was back in a lumber camp. He punched and kicked Tommy for two rounds.

Black boxer Billy Woods was advising Tommy from the corner during the bout. Before round three, Tommy gasped, "This guy's going to kill me if I don't knock him out."

"If you knock him out, this crowd is going to kill us both," Billy answered.

Minutes later, Klondike Mike kicked Tommy in the pit of his stomach. The blow sent Tommy reeling. He could not move for two minutes. Klondike Mike had won by a knockout.

Tommy had not come to Alaska to

The Nome Gold Rush

In 1898, three miners discovered gold in Alaska's Anvil Creek. About 10,000 people flooded into the area in the next year. Millions of dollars in gold was found in the sandy beaches on the Alaskan coast. The town of Nome sprang up quickly. At the height of the gold rush, Nome was home to 20,000 people.

fight. He was eager to reach his gold mine and start digging up gold. Tommy borrowed money so he could get started and hired Billy to join him on the trip. The pair headed out to Anvil Creek.

As they neared the mine, Billy sensed that someone was trailing them. He caught sight of men hiding in the bushes. Knowing that thieves were common, Billy and Tommy ran to the nearby mine and waited for the attack.

Soon, two armed men came into view. "This is a holdup! Come out with your hands up and nobody will get hurt!"

But Tommy had a surprise for the robbers. He held the gun that he had bought in Chicago. Scared and shaking, he fired at one of the men. His shot missed.

The thieves shot back with their rifles. When they stopped to reload, Tommy fired off all five of his rounds. He didn't hit the bandits, but the hail of bullets scared them. They ran away, leaving Tommy and Billy hiding in the mine.

The terrified boxers did not know where the thieves were. Stuck together in the mine overnight, Tommy and Billy became friends. They decided to meet in a bout if they made it home alive.

The next day, Tommy and Billy got to work. The deep, narrow mineshaft was a miserable place. Digging in the frozen ground was hard, and there was no gold to

Nome, Alaska in the early 1900s

be found. Tommy's career as a gold miner was a failure.

The boxers returned to Nome and sold the mine. It was time to leave Alaska, but Tommy had no place to go. He was banned from boxing in Detroit. He was scared to go back to Chicago. Billy convinced Tommy to try living in Billy's hometown — Los Angeles, California.

8 Love and Hate

A pit stop on the way from Nome to Los Angeles changed Tommy's life. The 23-year-old got off his steamship in Portland, Oregon. While onshore, he went with some friends to a dancehall. Inside, Tommy saw a tall and smartly dressed young woman. When she noticed him staring, he crossed the room and asked her to dance.

Tommy and Julia Keating soon became a couple. His friends were amazed that he was as interested in her as he was in boxing. Tommy and Julia married shortly after they met and settled in Los Angeles. As a play on his wife's name, and to show how lucky he felt to have her, Tommy called her Jewel.

Jewel was a proper lady. She never once watched Tommy in the ring. "I do hate fighting. You don't know how it affects my nerves … I was in bed for three weeks after one tilt," she complained. Tommy had to phone Jewel after each match to let her know that he was okay.

Jewel's family approved of her marrying a prizefighter. But they did not want him to fight black boxers. The Keatings were from the South and they did not treat black people as equals. When Tommy brought Billy Woods home for a meal, Jewel hissed, "It's okay to have them in the gym, but there'll be no coloureds in this house!"

Tommy did not listen to his wife or her family. As long as he was paid well, he would fight anyone. And he wouldn't give up his friends, black or white. Tommy kept his promise to meet Billy in a match. It was held in Seattle on September 16, 1904. It appeared to be an even matchup. The men were about the same height and weight. Both had great records. It was anyone's guess who would win.

The prizefighters boxed their best. Billy didn't seem to feel Tommy's hits. Tommy blocked Billy's punches. The match went the full 15 rounds. At the end, the referee declared a draw.

During the match, Tommy had yelled racist slurs at his friend. It was a common tactic used by white boxers, but Tommy regretted doing it. He told Billy that he was sorry. Billy replied, "I'm just thankful that you agreed to fight me; most whites won't come near me."

After the fight, Tommy asked Billy out for dinner. Tommy did not want a repeat of what had happened when he tried to dine with Harry Peppers. The restaurants close by were for whites only. The two men decided to eat at a place run by African-Americans. It was a daring move for Tommy. Jewel would not have been pleased if she found out.

From Seattle, Tommy took the train to Milwaukee, Wisconsin, to fight Hugo Kelly. But when Tommy arrived in the city, he learned that Kelly had been replaced with another fighter. "Philadelphia Jack" O'Brien was a boxing legend. He had been in 133 prizefights — Tommy had been in just 36. Plus, Philadelphia Jack was taller, heavier, and had longer arms than Tommy.

Tommy was not ready to take on Philadelphia Jack. The young boxer protested about the unfair matchup. "O'Brien will go easy and give the crowd a nice, friendly show," the promoter promised. Tommy agreed to fight on those terms.

But Philadelphia Jack was not friendly. He fought to win. The prizefighters exchanged blows for six rounds, and Tommy lost the match on points. Tommy felt betrayed by Philadelphia Jack, who joined Battleship Walsh on his list of foes. The fight soured Tommy on boxing for a while. He did not fight again for over three months.

Los Angeles was small and dull in the early 1900s. Tommy described it as "a big Hanover, without the snow." He spent a lot of time away from home, and Jewel was left behind. The year 1905 began with Tommy heading to the state of Washington for two fights. He won the first match with yet another knockout. Then he rested and trained for two months before facing Jack "Twin" Sullivan. Twin was good — he had fought Philadelphia Jack O'Brien to a draw.

The *London Free Press* described the fight that took place on March 7, 1905, as "one of the fastest ever seen in the state." A full 20 rounds flew by. Tommy and Twin were evenly matched, and the bout ended in a draw. Tommy didn't get to add a win to his record, but his skills created a buzz.

One of the people interested in Tommy was Dave Barry. He was the United States Pacific Coast champ. Like Tommy, Barry dreamed of winning a world title. A high-profile match with Tommy could help Barry get attention from the world champion. Maybe the champ would decide to box the winner.

Tommy and Barry agreed to fight in San Francisco, California. They worked out in the same club before the fight. At first, Tommy and Barry got along well. Then Barry met Jewel and began flirting with her. Maybe he was interested in Jewel, or maybe he was trying to make

Tommy lose his temper. Either way, Tommy got jealous. When Barry invited Jewel back to his place, Tommy swore he would tear Barry apart.

Tommy's fury showed when the boxers got into the ring. Opponents usually tapped each other's gloves before a match as a sign of respect. But Tommy refused to tap gloves with Barry. The battle that followed was brutal. For 20 rounds, they traded blows. Finally, the referee gave the win to Tommy based on points. Barry cried out that he should have won, but the crowd sided with the referee.

Tommy now held the United States Pacific Coast title, his first major win using his new name. His standing in the sports world took a great leap forward. Better boxers wanted to fight him and promoters paid more for title bouts. Tommy was on his way back to being a "somebody."

And he was free to fight in Michigan

again. A year had passed since he was banned by order of the police. On June 7, Tommy faced Hugo Kelly in Detroit. Kelly had backed out of their fight in Milwaukee. Now that Tommy had a title, Kelly wanted to take him on.

Kelly had actually beaten the great Philadelphia Jack. But Tommy had more on his mind than whether he was safe in the ring with Kelly. Hours before the match, Tommy was over the 72.5-kg

Blubberweight

Jewel's cooking made Tommy pack on weight. "Blubberweight" became his nickname in the press. At times, he was almost 13 kg (30 pounds) too heavy to box as a middleweight. Tommy often had to lose weight before a match. It hurt him in the ring and harmed his body.

(160-pound) limit for the middleweight division. With amazing speed, he worked off the weight. But it ruined him for the fight. After ten rounds, the referee announced a draw. Tommy and Kelly both wanted a clear-cut win. They agreed to face each other again the next month in Los Angeles.

The same train carried both men south to California. Fans at the rematch said that Tommy was the better boxer. However, like the first fight, it ended in a draw. The boxers called it quits and Tommy held on to the United States Pacific Coast title.

Dave Barry still believed that the Pacific Coast title should be his. He hounded Tommy, mocking the champ's record. Tommy had won just two of his last seven fights. Barry wanted a rematch. Tommy was up for the challenge.

The fight took place on the last day of August in 1905. It went 20 rounds. Tommy still hated Barry — he had gone too far with Jewel. Tommy always tried to be a gentleman, but that night he fought dirty. He held Barry by the neck and punched him. The referee did not seem to notice. In the last round, Tommy hit Barry with non-stop blows to the head. Barry finally fell to the ground, down for the count. Tommy never fought Dave Barry again.

9 King of the Ring

In late 1905, Tommy fought Twin Sullivan for the second time. Seven months had gone by since their last match. Twin was now calling himself the world middle-weight champ. After the last champ had retired, both Twin and Stanley Ketchel claimed the title. Instead of fighting for it, each man just announced that he was the new champ.

If Tommy could beat Twin, he would get a share in the title. Then he could take on Ketchel. Tommy was just two wins away from being the world middleweight boxing champion. But first he had to deal with Twin.

Tommy was once again too heavy to fight for his weight class. Before the weigh-in, Tommy starved himself. He got down to 71.6 kg (158 pounds) by the day of the bout, but he had left himself with no energy. The match was a letdown. Tommy was able to go the distance, but Twin won on points.

Tommy had a huge decision to make

Winning Isn't Everything

Although Tommy didn't have many wins in 1905, the money was good. He made more than $6,000. The sum was about ten times more than most people made in a year. And Tommy had boxed in only seven fights.

before his next match. His weight was hurting his career. He had to eat less or move to a new weight class. He could box as a light heavyweight if he stayed under 80 kg (175 pounds). But Tommy aimed higher. He became a heavyweight and joined the best boxers in the world. There would be no weight limit to trip him up now.

Tommy made his move soon after heavyweight champ Jim Jeffries retired. A favourite with fans and reporters, Jeffries was big, skilled, and undefeated. Now he wanted out. He admitted, "Fighting is not what it's cracked up to be."

Jeffries did not let other fighters argue over who would get his title. He planned a match to choose the new champ from among the white boxers he thought worthy. On July 5 in Reno, Nevada, Marvin Hart became the world heavyweight champ.

Many champs did a funny thing after winning. They stopped fighting, not wanting to risk their titles by meeting contenders. Hart went half a year before boxing again. In his first match as champ, he knocked out an unknown boxer in the first round.

A lot of men wanted to get in the ring with Hart. But he was looking for a certain kind of boxer.

"This guy's a lemon. I'll fight him next." That guy was Tommy.

Tommy's first fight as a heavyweight would be a huge one for him. If he won, he would be the champ! But Twin Sullivan had just beaten him. Tommy's career would be in trouble if he lost again. And it would not be easy to defeat Hart. The 29-year-old champ was 188 cm (6 feet 2 inches) and he weighed about 90 kg (200 pounds). In Hart's six-year career, he had lost just three fights.

Tommy decided that he would face Hart — but only if the price was right. Promoter Tom McCarey offered Tommy $15,000, a huge sum in 1906. "I'll take it," said the young boxer.

But McCarey could not come up with the money. He agreed to share the ticket sales instead. Tommy wanted to split the cash evenly with Hart, but the champ had another plan — 70 percent to the winner and 30 percent to the loser. Hart got his way.

No one seemed to care about the fight. It was "not causing the interest that a battle of its importance should ... there is no reason why [Hart] should not knock out his smaller opponent within 10 rounds," reported the *London Free Press*.

Jeffries, the former champ, got right to the point: "Hart will tear him to pieces. That Canadian shrimp won't last to hear the bell for round two."

Still, the two boxers took the match seriously. Tommy and Hart both trained as if their careers depended on it. Tommy needed an edge, so he hired Twin Sullivan as a spy. Twin watched Hart at the gym and reported back to Tommy. Through Twin, Tommy learned that Hart had a short temper and his footwork was slow.

Twin helped Tommy work out a plan. Hart was strong, so Tommy had to avoid his punches. Tommy would need to move fast in the ring. A few verbal jabs might also help Tommy. If Hart was angry, he could become careless.

Four thousand people packed into the Pacific Athletic Club on February 23, 1906. They were there to watch Hart thrash Tommy. When the boxers met in the ring, Hart saw that Tommy had put a lot of tape on his hands. The champ ordered Tommy to remove the extra tape.

Tommy nudged him and said, "Why,

Mr. Hart, I didn't think a big champion like you would mind that a little man like me used a little bit of tape."

Hart overreacted — just as Tommy hoped he would. The champ took a swing at Tommy before the fight even started. The crowd turned on Hart. It looked like he was bullying the smaller boxer. Back in his corner, Tommy was pleased. So far, his plan to annoy Hart was working.

When the bell rang, Tommy began to dance around the ring. He had to avoid getting hit. During the fifth round, Tommy got in a good punch of his own to Hart's right eye. The skin around the eye began to swell. Soon Hart could see from his left eye only. Tommy stayed to Hart's right, out of the champ's range of sight.

Hart's face became a bloody mess as the fight wore on. It looked as if Tommy would win on points. Hart would have to knock out Tommy to keep his title, but

Tommy stayed low and moved quickly. By the end of the 20 rounds, Tommy was still on his feet. He had won 18 of the rounds.

"My fight may not have been spectacular, but I wanted to win and fought the way I knew I could turn the trick. Hart didn't hurt me once," said Tommy.

The boxing world was in shock. Tommy Burns was the world heavyweight champion.

Tommy was not a well-liked champ in the United States. Americans were unhappy that a Canadian took the crown. The press looked like fools for backing Hart. But the worst was yet to come.

After his victory, Tommy made a shocking statement to reporters: "I will defend my title as heavyweight champion of the world against all comers, none barred. By this I mean white, black, Mexican, Indian, or any other nationality."

Tommy also made it clear that he would

Tommy wearing his world heavyweight championship belt

not try to keep the title in the United States. He wanted to be a true world champion. He looked forward to the fights he would get. They would help him become a better boxer. And the more he fought, the more money he would make.

Hart wanted a rematch but the champ turned him down. Their fight had been fair. Tommy wanted to test his skills against others. He had a lot to prove. Both the light-heavyweight and middleweight champs had defeated Tommy in the ring. But Tommy had faced Philadelphia Jack O'Brien and Twin Sullivan as a middleweight. He had worked so hard to shed the pounds that he didn't have the energy to beat them.

Tommy couldn't afford to make mistakes like that in the future. He had to train hard and be smart to protect his new title — and prove himself worthy of it.

10 Playing By the Rules

Three years earlier Tommy had fought two men in one night. He decided to try to pull it off again. But there was a lot more on the line this time.

On March 28, 1906, Tommy would defend his world heavyweight title for the first — and then second — time. The fights took place in San Diego, California. It was a good night for Tommy. After just two minutes and 18 seconds, he knocked out his first opponent. The second contest ended almost as fast as the first one.

The wins did not impress the media. The men Tommy beat were not viewed as real contenders. It would take much more to get the press behind Tommy. He had to find a heavyweight who would be truly difficult to beat.

"Fireman Jim" Flynn was taller and about 9 kg (20 pounds) heavier than Tommy. Fireman Jim also had a great record. He had done well against both Twin Sullivan and Philadelphia Jack O'Brien. A win against Fireman Jim was just what Tommy needed. A fight was planned for the first week in October.

Everyone wanted to see the fight between Tommy and Fireman Jim. Eight hundred fans were turned away from the packed Los Angeles arena. The boxers did not disappoint those who made it inside. This match was not going to end in a first–

round knockout. At first, Fireman Jim seemed to have the upper hand. Tommy kept at it, though. He slowly took control of the match.

The end came in round 15. Tommy knocked down Fireman Jim. The referee got to the count of nine before the dazed man rose. The same thing happened a second time. Then, with a flurry of right uppercuts, Tommy knocked down Fireman Jim for a third time. It was clear that Flynn was out for good. He did not get back on his feet for ten minutes.

At last, fans were impressed with the world champ. They rose to their feet and cheered for Tommy. It was his first standing ovation.

Tommy enjoyed his victory, but he did not take a break from the action. That November, an old foe challenged Tommy. Philadelphia Jack had beaten the champ once before. If he did it again, he could take the heavyweight title. After Tommy had lost their so-called exhibition match in 1904, he wrote, "*Get Jack O'Brien*" in his journal. Now he had a chance to do it.

The Burns-O'Brien fight was in Los Angeles. Most people were betting on Philadelphia Jack. He had 96 wins and just four losses. Even the referee — former heavyweight champ Jim Jeffries — openly backed the challenger.

It was a huge night. Philadelphia Jack held the light heavyweight title. Tommy met the lower division's weight limit, so both of the boxers' titles were on the line. Whoever won would be the light heavyweight and the heavyweight champ.

The men began to argue as soon as they met in the ring. Fans grew annoyed as they waited for the match to begin. After 15 minutes, Jeffries restored order and the fight began.

Tommy was out for blood, and he got it. In round five, he broke his enemy's nose. A punch to Philadelphia Jack's jaw almost knocked him out in the eighth round. The violence continued to the end of the match. Many people in the crowd thought that Tommy had won three-quarters of the rounds. It looked as if the heavyweight champ would take home two titles.

But Jeffries surprised everyone. He called it a draw.

"I am very well pleased with the decision," said Philadelphia Jack. "Jeffries did the right thing." He also admitted that Tommy "surprised me and showed that he is a dangerous opponent for any man."

His rival's praise was not good enough for Tommy. He was furious. "I won fairly and I think the decision was bad … Just compare our faces and draw your own conclusions."

Tommy hounded the new champ for a rematch. Philadelphia Jack was not keen to get back in the ring with him. Their fight had left Philadelphia Jack badly injured. But, in time, Tommy wore down his foe. They set up a meeting to plan a third bout.

When they met, Philadelphia Jack made Tommy an offer. "If you lie down you can have the whole purse — $10,000."

Philadelphia Jack wanted Tommy to throw the fight. The room was quiet as Tommy thought about it. Finally, Tommy replied, "You've got yourself a deal." Later, he handed over a bond of $1,000 to seal the pact.

But Tommy did not intend to throw the fight. He went along with the plan only to get Philadelphia Jack into the ring. Tommy was going to fight to win. The cash bond Philadelphia Jack held was fake. It was his turn to be betrayed.

On May 8, 1907, the rivals fought for the last time. Ten minutes before the match, Tommy spoke with the promoter and told him about the deal to throw the fight. The referee was asked to relay a message from the ring. "Gentlemen, all bets made on O'Brien to win up to this moment are off."

Tommy had Philadelphia Jack right where he wanted him. "Fight your best, Jack … I've got you here at last. This is a real fight."

Philadelphia Jack would not leave his corner to begin the match. He had to be pushed into the ring. The boxers went the whole 20 rounds. Philadelphia Jack spent most of his time running from Tommy. Whenever Tommy could, he showered Philadelphia Jack with punches. Tommy had finally got Jack O'Brien, just as he had written in his journal.

Tommy could have taken the light

heavyweight belt from Philadelphia Jack, but he said, "Forget it. I don't want that thing. Let O'Brien keep it." It did not matter. Belt or no belt, the heavyweight champion was now also the light heavyweight champ.

After the Fight

Philadelphia Jack was never able to repair his reputation. He fought in just a few more matches and then left boxing forever. Tommy turned down all offers to fight for the light heavyweight title. He wanted people to see him as the heavyweight champ — and nothing less. Five years after Tommy beat Philadelphia Jack, it was decided that the light heavyweight title was free for the taking. Hugo Kelly won it.

11 Fighting For Respect

Tommy's prize money made him rich by the time he was 25. In 1906, he and Jewel moved into a chic part of Los Angeles. Over time, Tommy bought a pub, a share in an art company, and even a farm. The rich and famous came to the Burns's parties. Tommy was a long way from his childhood poverty.

Back in Ontario, Tommy bought his mom her own house. She knew now that her son would not stop boxing. She even said that she would have liked to have seen one of Lil Noah's — Tommy's — bouts.

But something was missing. Tommy did not feel like a world champion. He craved respect. At the start of his career, he had been humble. People noted how polite the young boxer was. Now Tommy's head was as swelled as his body had become.

The champ came up with a new scheme to get the people on his side. He would do what no boxer had done before. Tommy would knock out "Iron Joe" Grim.

Iron Joe's record wasn't what drew crowds. Out of 400 or so fights, he had won about ten. Fans came to see the Italian fighter because he did not seem to feel pain. After each contest, Iron Joe cried, "I am Joe Grim! I fear no man on earth!" Indeed, none of the boxing greats had been able to get him down for the count. They won the matches through points.

The Burns–Grim match took place on January 10, 1907. Iron Joe did his trademark roll over the ropes and into the ring. His antics stopped when he saw how determined Tommy was — Iron Joe knew he was in trouble. He demanded that the rounds be shorter than the standard three minutes. Tommy wanted a knockout badly. He agreed to three one-minute-long rounds.

Tommy did the best he could with just three minutes. He knocked down Iron Joe five times during the brief match. But Iron Joe kept jumping back up for more abuse. Although Tommy won the match, fighting Iron Joe — who ended his days in a mental hospital — did nothing to help his image.

But Tommy found another way to win fans. At the time, heavyweight champs took part in variety shows. Tommy travelled from place to place showing off his boxing skills. The crowds loved him.

"Klondike" Haynes toured with Tommy. They sparred onstage and worked out together. The champ did not seem to care that Klondike was black. They even roomed together.

The champ never forgot what it was like to be poor. While on the road, he was kind toward others who were in need. Tommy talked about his youth during a charity show at Christmas. People cried as they heard his story.

Tommy got plenty of attention while he was away from home. He also ate a lot. The heavyweight became truly heavy. The weight gain put his boxing career at risk. "They can say what they like, but theatrical work is the worst thing in the world for a fighter," he said.

As Tommy grew fat, the press' attention was elsewhere. The heavyweight champ of Australia, Bill Squires, was in California. Squires challenged Jim Jeffries to a fight, but had no interest in Tommy. "I have come half way around the world to fight this man Jeffries and will not be put off on anyone else," said Squires.

It seemed that no one in the boxing world held Tommy in high regard. But sportswriters loved Squires. He had never lost a fight. All but three of his 26 contests had been knockouts.

It did not matter how much Squires wanted a match with Jeffries. The retired boxer would not fight Squires. The Australian champ had to settle for a match with Tommy after all. The Burns-Squires fight was set for July 4, America's Independence Day. It would be up to 45 rounds long. The Canadian had to get in shape — fast.

As usual, Tommy learned as much as he could about his opponent. Squires was taller and heavier than Tommy. However, Tommy had speed and smarts. He studied

Jim Jeffries refereed the Burns-Squires fight on July 4, 1907. Burns is on the right.

Squires's skills. The bigger man was a powerful puncher. Tommy needed to dodge his blows.

Nine thousand fans came to the outdoor ring to watch the afternoon match. The crowd gathered under the hot sun. The roar of the voices was loud as the fight began.

Just into the first round, Tommy faked a punch and then jabbed his right fist into Squires's jaw. The Australian went down, but he was not out. Tommy quickly knocked down Squires again. But the bruised man pulled himself up to fight. Tommy punched Squires again and he fell a third time. This time he was down for the count.

The match had ended in less than three minutes. The many reporters who backed Squires quickly turned on him. A pattern had formed. Time after time, the press would praise Tommy's challengers and predict his defeat. When Tommy won, his rivals quickly became known as poor fighters.

Tommy knew why so many people were against him. The world heavyweight boxing champion was not meant to be a short Canadian. His ties with black boxers made it worse. No matter what Tommy did, most Americans would find something wrong with it.

12 Against All Comers

British Empire champ James "Gunner" Moir wanted Tommy's title. Tommy just wanted to fight. By 1907 he was running out of opponents. He kept setting up matches with big names, but the plans always fell through. Then the National Sporting Club invited Tommy to England. He would battle Gunner there.

England was wild about boxing. They considered it their sport. When Tommy arrived in London, he was a letdown. He did not look like a champion. The English did not think that he even looked like an athlete. Tommy commented, "Some of them were saying that I was too small ... others said, 'poor fellow, wait till the Gunner gets him.'"

Some English fans were rude to Tommy. One morning, when he was out for a run, he was pushed off the sidewalk — by a police officer. "The road's the place for you," said the officer.

The fall sprained Tommy's ankle. The prizefighter was angry, but he felt better when a group of officers was forced to apologize to him the next day.

The Burns–Moir fight was set for December 2, 1907. The posh National Sporting Club was unlike any place that Tommy had ever fought in. Men came to the match dressed in tuxedos. Talking was forbidden during the action. The crowd fell silent when the two men entered the ring.

Tommy yelled, "When I knock Moir down, I want the count to be out loud so everyone can hear it."

Gunner was clearly rattled.

At first, the boxers were cautious. By the end of the first round, Tommy had got in two hard punches to Gunner's head. In round two, Tommy took a blow under his chin. But by the fifth round, Tommy was in control. Blood began to flow from a gash above one of Gunner's eyes. He kept clinching to avoid being hit. The end came in round ten when Tommy punched a weakened Gunner again and again. Finally, the Englishman went down. He did not get up.

Tommy did not know what to expect from the crowd. He had knocked out their boxing hero. The English fans surprised Tommy when they stood up and began to cheer for the Canadian.

Tommy decided to stay in London.

The fight had made him a lot of money, and he already had plans for another match. The promise of cash always appealed to him.

In February 1908, the champ fought Britain's second-best boxer, Jack Palmer. English fans hoped that this time their man would wind up with the world title. But Palmer went down in the fourth round.

The next month, Tommy visited Ireland. He prepared to defend his title again against Jem Roche, Ireland's champ. Tommy and Roche were set to meet on St. Patrick's Day.

The challenger's manager claimed, "Jem is just the sort to make a world's champion — strong, fast, clever, cool, and determined … I fail to see how Jem can lose." The Irish public agreed.

On the night of the bout, Tommy felt good. He was so sure of himself, he made a hefty bet that he would return to his hotel in time for dinner — just half an hour after the fight was to begin.

Boxing fans flooded the city of Dublin. More than 3,000 people jammed into the theatre where the ring was set up. They cheered for Roche and booed at Tommy. He shut them up quickly. Just one minute and 28 seconds into the first round, Tommy knocked out the Irishman. The champ helped Roche back to his corner.

"I'm not beat, am I, Mr. Burns?" Roche asked.

Tommy replied, "I'm afraid you are, Jem."

One of the people watching the fight ran outdoors as soon as it ended. He yelled to the crowd, "I can't bear to look at it. Roche is murdering him. Is there anyone here who could bear to witness the horrid spectacle? He can buy my ticket for two pounds."

The trickster was not the only one to profit on the short match. Tommy dashed back to his hotel. He made it to dinner and won his bet.

That spring, back in London, Tommy agreed to fight the world amateur boxing champ. Johnny Douglas and Tommy would meet in an exhibition match. Tommy's title was not on the line, but Douglas fought as if it was. Tommy was not prepared. It was a tough fight, but it was just an exhibition bout so no winner was declared.

"If this is what you call a sparring exhibition, what is your honest-to-God fighting like down here?" joked Tommy after the bout. He was actually angry. Like Philadelphia Jack O'Brien, Douglas had gone back on his word to take it easy. But Tommy let it go. He didn't need any more enemies. Plus, there was still money to be made.

Just four days later, Tommy fought South African Joseph Smith. The white

African boxer had been in only two big matches before he fought Tommy. But Tommy had promised to be a true world champion. The contest took place in Paris, France.

Before the match, Tommy played his usual mind games. When he met with Smith to sign the fight contract, Tommy tried to scare him. "Sign these contracts like a good fellah. Don't be a quitter. I'll let you stay a round or two," Tommy said. In fact, Tommy let Smith stay on his feet for five rounds before he knocked him out.

After his four wins, Tommy took a break. He and Jewel went on a month-long trip to Belgium, France, Germany, and the Netherlands. And Tommy had more travel plans. The Burnses would leave for Australia in August. The champ would defend his title on yet another continent.

13 Boxing Day

Few people knew the real reason Tommy
went to Australia in the summer of 1908.
It was not to give boxers there a shot at the
title. And it was not for the praise he
received from the fans. The 27-year-old
champ was there to fight Jack Johnson.

Johnson was not Australian. The black
boxer had been born in Texas to parents
who had been slaves.

In Johnson's youth, white men put on
fights that pitted black boys against each

other. Up to 12 of them fought at the same time. The boys were sometimes bound, blindfolded, or forced to take off their clothes. They fought for the pennies the crowd threw at them. Johnson won often. But the experience made him tough and bitter.

Four years after he became a prizefighter, Johnson had fought the great Joe Choynski. Boxing was illegal in Texas at the time, and both men were arrested. Johnson and Choynski spent three weeks in prison. They shared a cell, and Choynski drilled Johnson on boxing skills. The odd boot camp helped Johnson excel in the sport.

For years, Johnson challenged heavyweight champs to matches. They all drew the colour line. Then Tommy came along. In the autumn of 1907, before Tommy went to England to fight Gunner Moir, Johnson challenged him to a match. Jewel warned her husband that she would leave him if he kept fighting black boxers. Still, Tommy agreed to the fight. The world heavyweight title would be within reach of a boxer who was not white. The news rocked the sports world.

Johnson asked for half of the ticket sales. Tommy knew what he was worth — he wanted three-quarters of the profits. Johnson needed the fight more than Tommy did, so Tommy knew that he would get what he wanted if he waited.

The boxers still had not signed a contract when Tommy left for London. In the spring of 1908, Johnson arrived in England. He spread the word that Tommy was trying to avoid the fight. Around the world, people became more and more interested in the matchup. Finally, Tommy got what he wanted: an offer of $30,000 to fight Johnson. It was the most money that a boxer had ever made for a fight.

Promoter Hugh McIntosh wanted to keep up the hype. The time and place of the fight — Sydney, Australia, on December 26, 1908 — and the details of the deal were kept secret. Tommy had just one thing to do. He had to keep his title. If he lost it, the fight would be off — and he would be paid nothing.

While in Paris, Tommy had fought Bill Squires for a second time. The Australian did much better than he had in their first match. But Tommy had won with a knockout in the eighth round. After arriving in Australia, Tommy agreed to fight Squires a third time. Tommy's unannounced match with Johnson was still months away.

The Burns-Squires bout on the Australian's home turf had fans excited. About 20,000 people showed up for the sold-out fight on August 24. Tommy was just getting over the flu. He was in rough shape. Squires took nine of the first 11 rounds. Because his title match with Johnson was a secret, Tommy was one of the few people who knew what was really on the line. He had to get punching — and he did. By round 13, Squires was in trouble. After two knock downs, Tommy knocked out Squires for the third and final time. Australian newspapers began calling Tommy the "Little Giant."

Tommy and Jewel travelled around the country while waiting for his big fight to be announced. Sportswriters claimed that he was lying low. The champ could not explain why he was not heading back to fight Johnson in the United States. Finally, Hugh McIntosh announced the Burns-Johnson fight. The world heavyweight boxing champion would be decided on Boxing Day.

In October, Johnson arrived in Australia. He taunted Tommy. "How does Burns

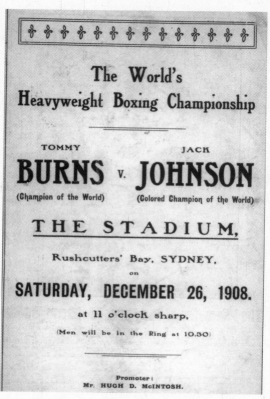

The colour line is seen in this poster for the Burns-Johnson championship match. Johnson is labelled the "Colored Champion of the World."

want it? Does he want it fast and willing? I'm his man in that case. Does he want it flat-footed? Goodness, if he does, why I'm his man again. Anything to suit; but fast or slow, I'm going to win."

Tommy was worried. He admitted privately, "I will give him the fight of his life, although I don't think I can beat him."

Johnson was almost 18 cm (7 inches) taller and about 9 kg (20 pounds) heavier than Tommy. Plus, the champ was sick again. He spent the week before the big fight in bed. Doctors were not sure what was wrong with him. It might have been another case of the flu. But, flu or not, Tommy would box. McIntosh would not delay the fight.

The outdoor arena was packed on Boxing Day. Thousands of fans stood outside, hoping to get tickets. Just before 11:00 in the morning, Tommy and Johnson were introduced to the crowd.

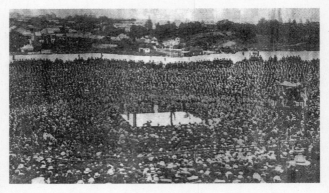

Thousands of fans showed up for the Burns-Johnson championship match.

The fighters had up to 20 rounds of boxing ahead of them. At 11:07, the bell rang to start the fight.

Neither man held back. The punches flew. They clinched so that neither could get in a hit. To break them up, the referee held Tommy's glove. Johnson quickly swung an uppercut at the champ. The upward punch knocked Tommy to the ground.

Tommy evened the score with a punch

that threw back Johnson's head. The challenger seemed undisturbed. He called out, "Poor little Tommy, did someone kid you you were a fighter?" By the end of the first round, Johnson was in control. He would not stop smiling.

By round three, Tommy knew he was in trouble. He stayed low to block Johnson's punches. Tommy got in a few good blows

Boxing Day or Bust

McIntosh chose the date for the Burns-Johnson fight very carefully. The promoter knew that three huge American warships would be in Sydney on December 26. About 4,000 sailors would be looking for something to do while their ships were docked. A match for the world heavyweight title would attract most of them — as well as thousands of Australian fans.

Jack Johnson was the first black man to box in a world heavyweight championship fight.

of his own. He even managed to win the round. Small and sick, Tommy did his best to defend himself against Johnson.

The men kept trading blows. Both were bruised and bleeding. By the tenth round, the boxers were slowing down. Johnson was ahead in the points, but his ribs may have been broken. His team wanted to end the match.

The "Little Giant" met his match in Johnson.

Someone from Johnson's corner slipped into the crowd. He began chanting, "Stop the fight. Stop the fight." Fans took up the chant. "Stop the fight!"

The police were paying close attention. They thought Tommy was in danger. At the end of the round, they warned the referee that they were ready to step in. Tommy did not want them to end the fight. He thought that Johnson was slowing down.

In round 14, Johnson rushed at Tommy. A strong punch to the head knocked Tommy to the ground. He was not out, though. Tommy stood up. Then to his surprise, the police entered the ring.

For Tommy's safety, the police decided to end the bout. Tommy begged to keep fighting. But the police claimed that he was too injured to go on. They may have been trying to prevent a riot — the likely result if a black man knocked out a white man. The fight ended and the referee gave the win to Johnson. He took the match and the world heavyweight title.

14 Down and Out

Jack Johnson made history as the first black world heavyweight boxing champion. Tommy also made history. He went down as one of the worst boxers ever to hold the title. The media claimed that he stayed a champ by fighting only unskilled opponents. Tommy's speed and strength, his many knockouts, and the number of times he defended his title were all ignored.

Johnson also trashed Tommy, and would not fight him again. The new champ said,

"I have forgotten more about fighting than Burns ever knew." But Johnson hid that he had been in the hospital for a week after the title fight.

Only sportswriter Joe Jackson told the truth about his old friend Tommy. Joe wrote, "Burns is being blamed, not for losing his title, but for letting a negro have a chance at it."

Tommy threw away his gloves after he lost the title match. He stayed in Australia. This time he really was hiding. More than a year later, the former champ finally agreed to a fight. He had knocked out Billy Lang during a fight in 1908. Now Lang was the champion of the British Empire and he wanted a rematch. Tommy was not at his best, but he won the 20-round bout. Winning another title did not cheer up Tommy. He didn't even bother to defend it.

In the summer of 1910, Tommy went

back to the United States, where he and Jewel had a baby. In time, they had four daughters: Margaret, Patricia, Mary, and Helen. Tommy was crazy about his girls.

In his early thirties, Tommy began managing other boxers. Sportswriters were searching for the "Great White Hope," a white boxer who could beat Johnson. One of Tommy's fighters, Luther McCarty, was getting ready to take on the world champ.

But McCarty never got the chance to fight Johnson. A single punch in the first round of a match killed McCarty. The police charged Tommy with manslaughter because he had promoted the fight. The autopsy showed that McCarty had died because of an injury he got before the fight. It cleared Tommy's name. For a second time in his life, he was lucky to escape blame for another boxer's death.

Tommy boxed in just six more matches over the next decade. His final fight was on July 16, 1920. The referee ended it in round seven. Tommy lost his last fight the same way he lost his most important title fight — by appearing too injured to carry on.

Tommy moved a lot. He volunteered with the Canadian army during World War I. He was a fitness instructor for thousands of troops. Tommy also owned a sports arena and a clothing store in Calgary, Alberta, and bars in the United States and England.

He did well with his businesses and investments. And he still had plenty of prize money. He made about $209,000 during his boxing career. The same amount would be worth more than two million dollars today.

But hard times were ahead. Jewel had a mental illness. Tommy and Jewel tried to save their marriage, but they split up for good in 1920. Tommy got custody of his kids, and Jewel died a few years later.

Another huge blow to hit Tommy was the 1929 stock market crash. He lost most of his money, so he suddenly needed a job. And he wanted to return home to Canada. Tommy wrote to the country's Prime Minister asking for a job with the government and suggesting that he "would be a great asset." But the Canadian government turned him down.

Tommy moved to Texas and sold life insurance for a living. Later, he headed north to Washington state and became a security guard. His glory years may have been over, but he did gain something that he had always wanted. A man who knew Tommy then described him as having "the respect of everyone." He also fell in love again, this time with a widow named Nellie. He married for a third time at the age of 65.

As Tommy grew older, he turned to the faith of his youth. His dad's dream for him came true: Tommy became a minister in 1948. He visited and spoke in churches along the west coast of the United States. In the mid-1950s, Tommy spoke in a black Baptist church about the black boxer who had won his biggest title from him. He said that Jack Johnson had shown him that African-Americans were "as brave, as clever and as strong as anyone." Tommy called for the walls between the races to be "knocked down."

Tommy practised what he preached. The old champ said, "My main object in life is to help the sick and the suffering." He did whatever was asked of him, volunteering in hospitals, orphanages, and even prisons.

Then, in May 1955, Tommy went to Vancouver, British Columbia, to visit friends. Back in his home country, the 73-year-old had a fatal heart attack. None of his family or friends were able to attend the funeral. Tommy was buried in an unmarked grave set aside for the poor.

But the former champ was not forgotten. A group of Tommy's old friends wanted to honour him. They teamed up with a local sportswriter and raised money to buy a plaque. A graveside service took place six years after his death. "Nobody can take away from Tommy Burns what he did," a reverend told the crowd.

The year he died, Tommy was inducted into the Canadian Sports Hall of Fame and the Canadian Boxing Hall of Fame. The International Boxing Hall of Fame admitted Tommy as an "old-timer" in 1996. But there was more to Tommy than his success as an athlete.

Noah Brusso changed his name, but it seemed that he could not change his fate. No matter where he was or what he was called, the boy who would rather fight than eat was always the underdog. But he never gave up — he just worked harder.

Tommy was generous and committed to doing what was right. From creating an inner-city boxing club for boys to giving up his hotel room to a family he saved from a fire, Tommy was happy to help people in need.

He was also a smart businessman. Because of his deals with promoters, fighters started getting much larger shares of the profits.

Most important of all, Tommy was willing to cross the colour line and give black boxers a chance. Fighters like his friends Billy Woods and Harry Peppers, and even foes like Jack Johnson, were treated as equals because of Tommy.

The fans who loved him and the press who hated him could all agree on one thing: Tommy Burns changed the sport of boxing forever.

Glossary

Amateur: An athlete who participates for fun and is not paid

Bout: A boxing match that has one-minute breaks between a set number of rounds

Championship: A competition, or contest, for a title or prize

Clinch: When a boxer clutches an opponent to avoid being punched

Down for the count: When a knocked-down boxer is unable to get to his or her feet within ten seconds

Draw: A tie that is the result of opponents scoring the same number of points

Exhibition match: A sporting event that does not count toward rankings

Going the distance: A boxer's ability to make it through all the scheduled rounds

Heavyweight: In the early 1900s, boxers with no upper weight limit

Hook: A sideways punch done with the arm bent like a hook

Induct: To add as a member

Jab: A quick, sharp punch that shoots out from chin level

Knocked down: When a boxer touches the ground

with anything other than his or her feet, or is being held up by the ropes

Knockout: When a knocked-down boxer does not rise by the count of ten

Left hook: A hook done with the left fist

Lightweight: In the early 1900s, boxers up to 61 kg (135 pounds)

Match: A contest between two boxers

Middleweight: In the early 1900s, boxers up to 72.5 kg (160 pounds)

Opponent: The rival boxer, player, or team

Prizefighter: A boxer who fights for money

Professional: A person who is paid to work as an athlete

Referee: An official who makes sure that the rules of a sport are followed

Right cross: A punch delivered with the right fist as the upper body twists and the right foot turns

Round: A three-minute-long period when boxers fight in the ring

Undisputed: Something that is not questioned

Uppercut: An upward punch delivered at close range

Acknowledgements

Many sources claim that Tommy Burns was not a great champion. The media nearly ruined his reputation in the early 1900s. Fortunately, *Tommy Burns: Canada's Unknown World Heavyweight Champion* by Dan McCaffery makes it clear how great Tommy truly was. I am indebted to McCaffery for providing a wealth of information about Tommy. A lot of the dialogue in this book comes from personal interviews that McCaffery conducted with Tommy's family and friends.

I am also grateful to the writers of the

numerous books and articles that helped guide me to a better understanding of the sport. Thank you to the helpful staff at the Huntsville Public Library — hooray for interlibrary loans! Material from the *Globe and Mail*, the *London Free Press*, and the *Toronto Globe* helped bring Tommy to life. Video clips of Tommy in action are easy to find on the Internet and are well worth viewing to get a feel for how boxing has changed over the years.

I'd like to thank the team at Lorimer: Hadley Dyer, who got me started on this project; designer Meghan Collins; and the publishers, Chris Keen and Jim Lorimer. I especially appreciate all the work that children's book editor Faye Smailes and copy editor Kat Mototsune put into the book.

Finally, many thanks to Tim, Jane, Peter, Doreen, Bruce, and Gael for their interest in this book — and in me!

About the Author

REBECCA SJONGER is the author of twenty-five non-fiction books for children and young adults. Previously, she was the program coordinator at The Canadian Children's Book Centre. She lives in Huntsville, Ontario, with her family.

Photo Credits

Canadian Sports Hall of Fame: p 29

Jean Gateman: p 14, back cover bottom

Image Library, State Library of New South Wales: p 114, p 116, p 119, back cover middle

Library of Congress American Memory Collection: p 65

Dan McCaffery's collection: p 11, p 57, p 99, front cover top

National Archives of Canada: No. C14094 back cover top

Larry Roberts: p 84

Kevin Smith: p 118

Marquis Book Printing Inc.

Québec, Canada
2008